AFRO-BETS® ABC BOOK

by Cheryl Willis Hudson

apple

A a Africa

alligator

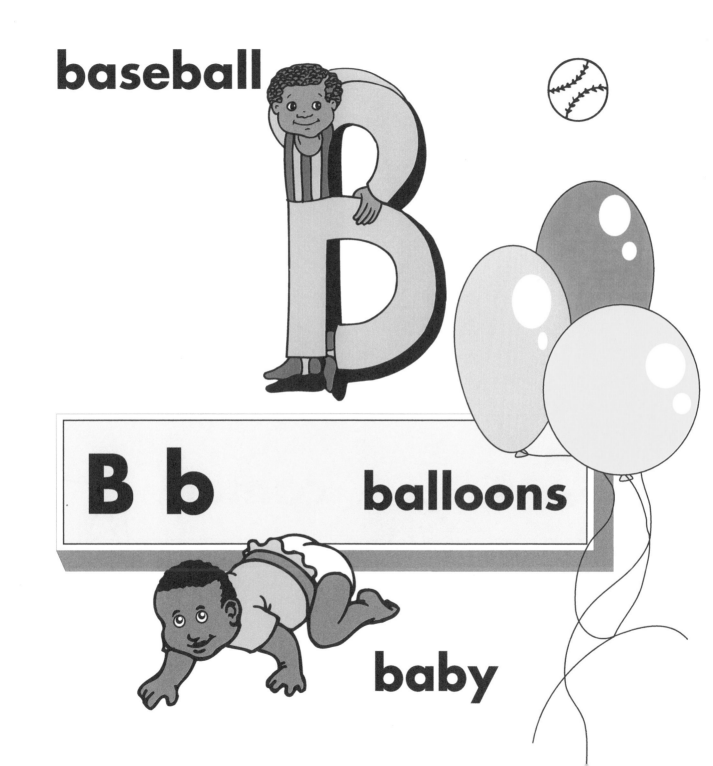

baseball

B

B b   balloons

baby

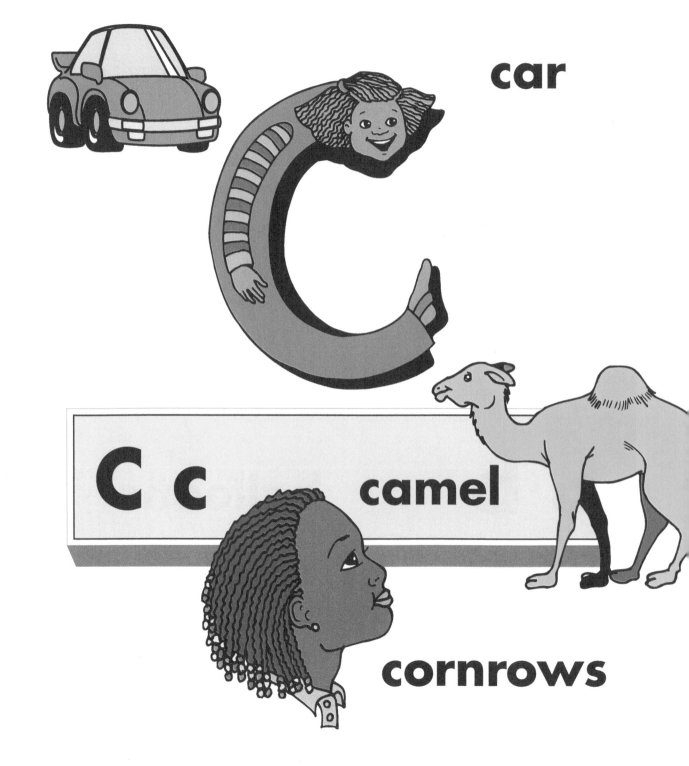

car

C c camel

cornrows

doll

D d   dog

dancers

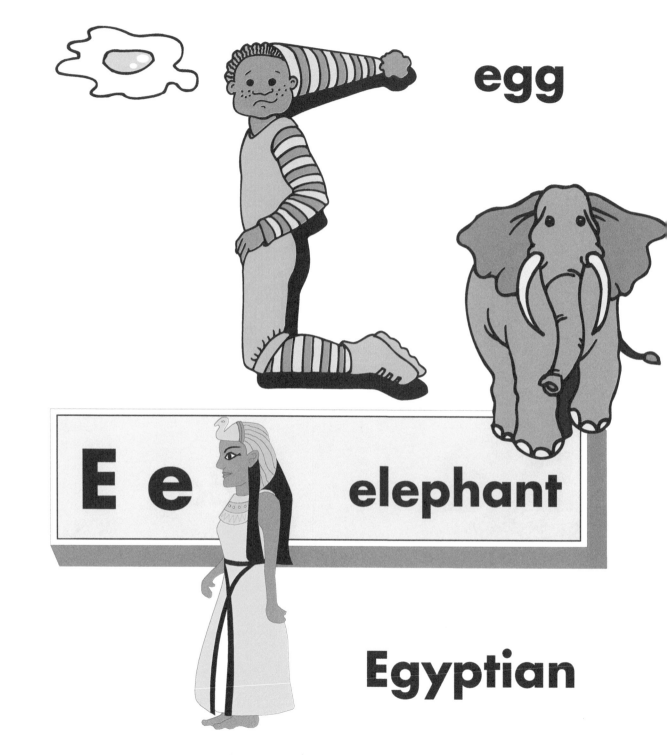

egg

elephant

Egyptian

E e

football

F f

feather

fish

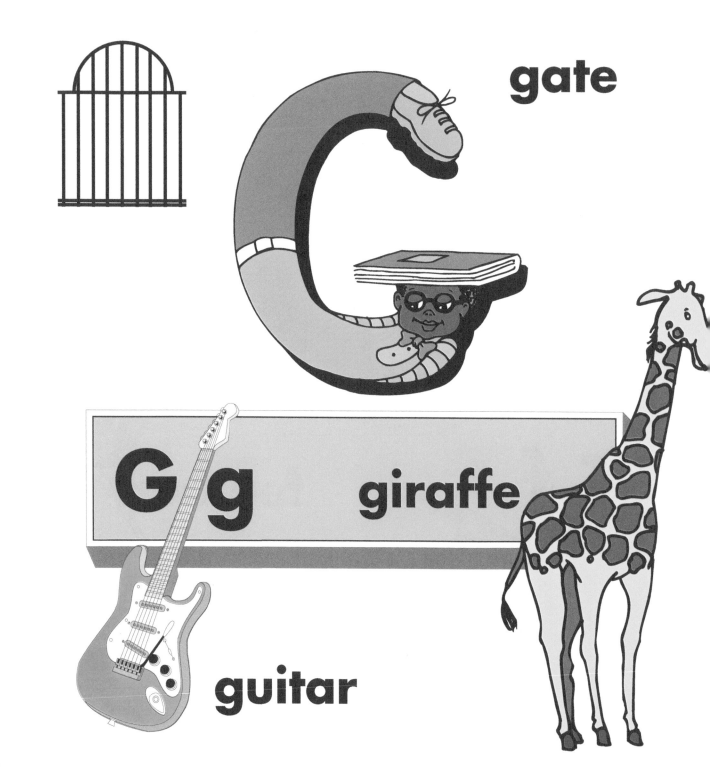

gate

G g

giraffe

guitar

hotdog

H h house

hippo

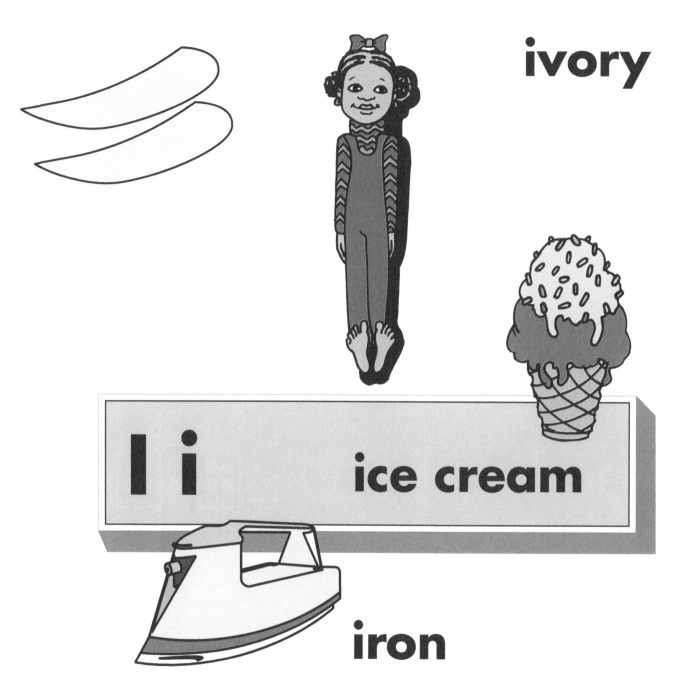

ivory

I i   ice cream

iron

jet

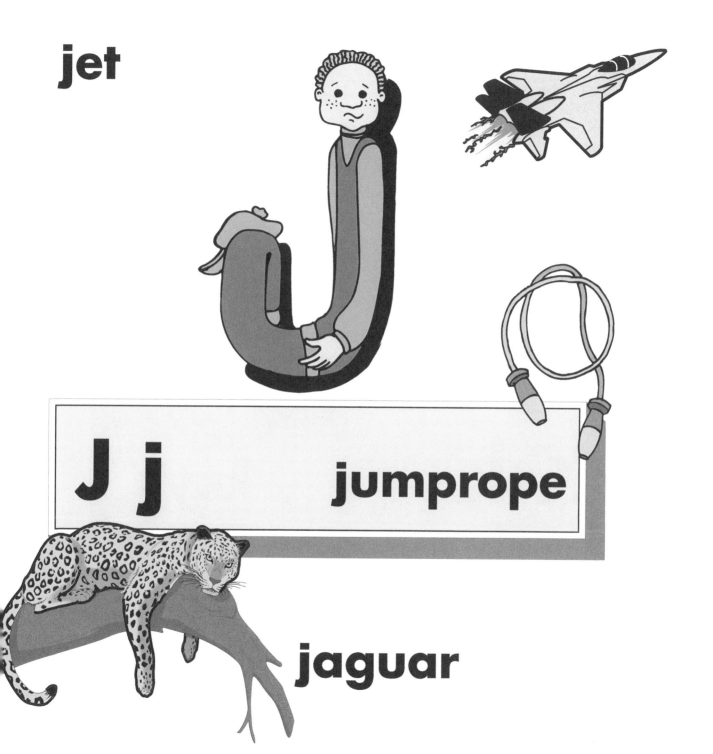

J j

jumprope

jaguar

kitten

keys

K k

Kente cloth

lips

L l

lion

ladybug

mask

monkey

M m

magician

nose

N n   Nefertiti

9 nine

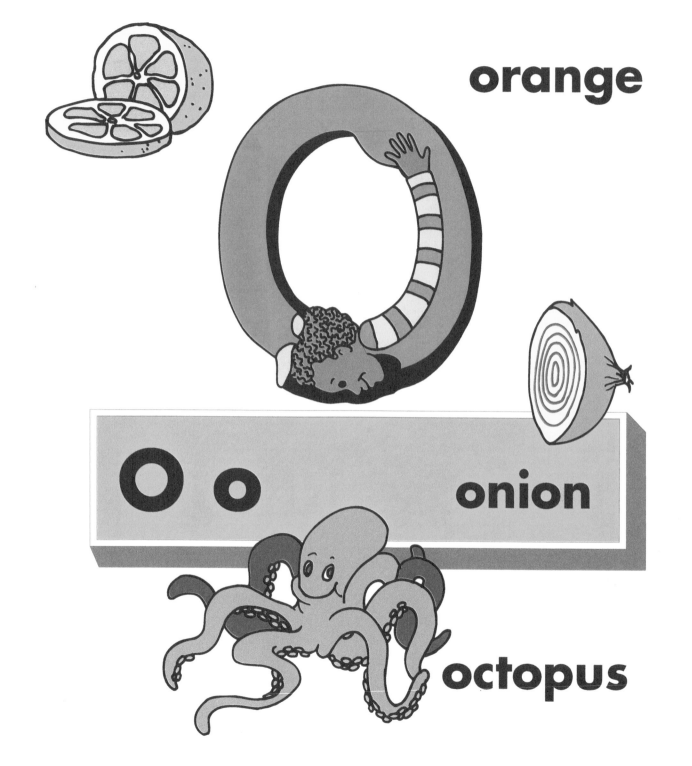

orange

onion

O o

octopus

peanuts

P p

pencil

panda

queen

Q q quilt

question mark

rose

R r   rainbow

rhinoceros

stop

S s

sun

sphinx

television

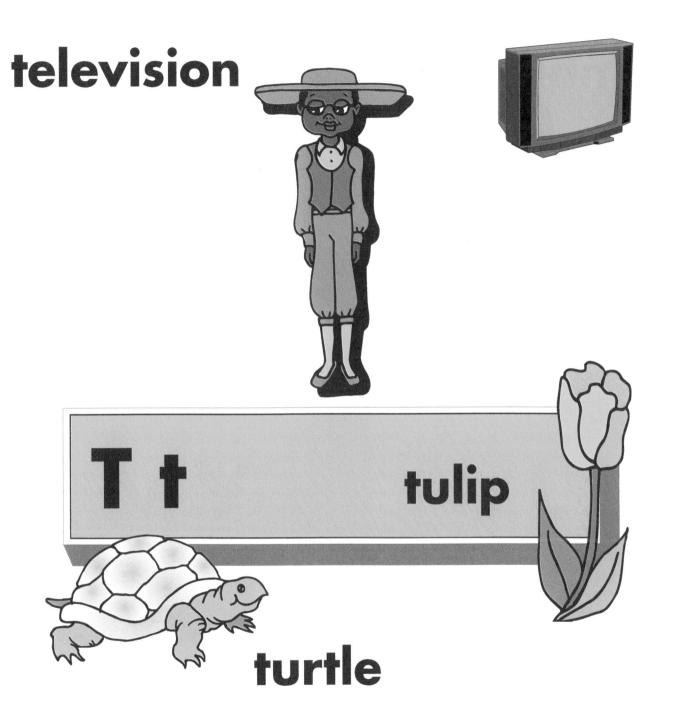

T t

tulip

turtle

umbrella

valentine

U u   **V v**

unicycle   **volcano**

window

xylophone

W w   X x

wagon   **x-ray**

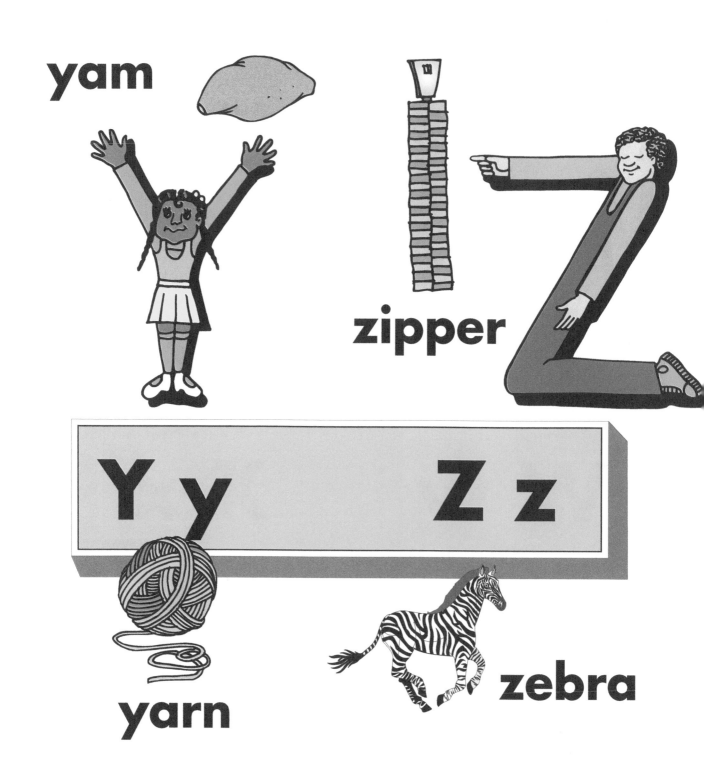

yam

zipper

Y y   Z z

yarn

zebra

CPSIA information can be obtained at www.ICGtesting.com
Printed in the USA
BVOW10s2250120815

413146BV00005B/5/P